Scarred

Healing and Moving Forward

By Jonathan E. Pariseau

Coauthors Kimberly J Pariseau and William Dunn

DORRANCE
PUBLISHING CO
EST. 1920
PITTSBURGH, PENNSYLVANIA 15238

Dorrance Publishing Co
585 Alpha Drive
Suite 103
Pittsburgh, PA 15238
Visit our website at *www.dorrancebookstore.com*

ISBN: 979-8-8860-4421-8
eISBN: 979-8-8868-3842-8

Dedication

I dedicate this book to my dear brotherly friend the late Steve "Ebie" Davis who married my "step" daughter, Brittany. I put step in quotes because her and her brother's father Russell Malone tells me "There is no step to it because we are all their parents." I am thankful to Brittany for bringing Steve along in her and my family's life journey over the past 14 to 15 years up until Steve took his last step in his earthly journey in March of this year 2022. He is now in his eternal journey. Steve is definitely the example of what a true husband, father, grandfather, son, and brother is. He has sisters but no brother, and while I have 15 brothers, he and I were very much like brothers, and that is how I will always remember him as my brotherly friend. God bless you, Ebie, as you travel on eternally.

Acknowledgements

I want to first recognize my wife, Kimberly Pariseau, who I have been traveling along with now for close to thirty years. In my 56-year journey, I have never been with any one person or in any one place than with Kim at our home and with our family. She has definitely learned more about my life than most and even helped me meet up with my baby brother who I haven't seen since the late sixties/early seventies.

I also want to thank my parents, the late Dennis and Donna Pariseau, for being the ones who figuratively reached out and grabbed me out of a chaotic, dangerous place and afforded me the opportunity to thrive in life. I have had the opportunity to consult with their friend, Mr. William Dunn, as I have written this book and appreciate all his support and advice.

I also want to recognize the different friends I have traveled along with at different times in my life journey up to now, beginning with my dear friend and comrade, Corissa Boggs, who I have traveled along with now for around 25 years. I thank her for introducing me to her aunt who I will not mention by name but you know who you are!!! I thank you like Mr. Dunn for your advice and support during this process.

I am thankful for my wonderful college friends LaRue Rogers now Neilson, James Whitecotton, Darryl Yates, Theresa Mayton now Herald, and Mark Collett. We had a lot of memorable times together and you all have in one way or another inspired me. Thank you very much!!!

Last but definitely not least I want to acknowledge some of my Shawnee Family Health Center's work family who I have traveled along with throughout my career at SFHC beginning of course with my very dear friend Corissa Boggs, Cynthia Holstein, John Bowman, Anita Bowman, Janie and Jim Haas, Gina Raynard, Patty Sparks, Roxanne Vice, Cyndy Bell, Kelly Montavon, David Atkins,

Elaine Evans and two of the younger members of the family Taylor Fyffe, and the newest member Kaitlin Colley who you will learn more about as you read on. I thank all of you for your influences in my life and also thank the many others who I haven't been able to mention.

Prologue

In my close to thirty-year career as a Social Worker, I have found myself discussing three things with people and that is: 1. Life journey, 2. Emotional scars (traumas), and 3. Death, which is sadly something most all of us have in common. We all have lost persons that are close to us.

In this book, I share my own life journey and talk about my own emotional scars as a way to explain figurative terms "life journey" and "emotional scars." The fact is a person's life journey begins at birth and ends at death, and for this reason, I also talk about how I have chosen to accept the losses of loved ones. It is my hope that by telling this story, anyone reading it can be helped in making sense of his or her life journey and the life journeys of others who have since gone onto their eternal journeys.

Footnote - On the inside of the cover, you will notice I am wearing the Bengals shirt I wore while watching the Super Bowl in February. I have been a lifelong Bengals fan, celebrated when they went to the Super Bowl in the eighties, and have remained a fan over the years, knowing that in their journey they would be the champions they were last year. I believe they will continue to play like champions and even return to the Super Bowl, and even more, win it before I take my last step in this journey called life.

Scarred

Healing and Moving Forward

By Jonathan E. Pariseau

Coauthors Kimberly J Pariseau and William Dunn

"We all have a life story to tell" are the words I heard one Sunday morning while in church. A very dear and special friend Corissa Boggs invited me, my wife, and family to church where my wife and I have since become members, and while my attendance record has been below average to be modest, I believe I was meant to hear those words that Sunday morning in 2021.

Pastor Rob Krebbs of Sciotoville Christ United Methodist went on to talk about his brother's struggles with addiction, which sadly we all probably know people who have had their own struggles in this area. His brother conquered and shared his journey and struggles with others who are in their own journey, and it was inspiring, helpful, and motivational to those persons.

As I thought about it, I, like everyone, have a story to tell and I am looking for a way to tell as many people as possible. I have lost track of the times from my teenage years, college years, and adult years up to now when people have told me, "you need to tell your story."

Now at age 56, I think about those words, "you need to tell your story," and I hear them differently. I hear I have a responsibility to tell others, and that I owe it to others especially if at least one person who isn't as far along in his/her life journey can hear something that can help them overcome traumas and truly live life to the fullest, and the sad fact is there continues to be children who are experiencing heartbreaking traumas.

Having raised three stepchildren, and having been there with my 18-year-old granddaughter from the start of her life journey, and walking along now with my seven-year-old grandson in his journey, I have come to realize that children are truly resilient.

You see, I have watched my grandchildren as little tikes taking off with a smile and running and then falling, crying, and me picking them up with scraped knees. Well, both grandchildren continued to run, and have become more coordinated and the falls became fewer and fewer. They have played sports like softball, baseball, volleyball, and basketball, and have enjoyed doing so.

Enjoying watching my stepchildren as they grew in their own life journeys and now my grandchildren, one thing I have always believed has been proven and that is most likely we all have a scar or two but have continued to travel on in life.

The good news for my grandchildren, great granddaughter, my stepdaughter, and stepson is that your journey isn't over, just as mine isn't either.

One day, you will be my age reflecting on your journeys, which are full of a lot more wonderful moments, and yes, some more sadness, disappointments, and heartbreaks as well, but I am sure you can do as you have done before, and that is get up with help from those who love and care about you, brush yourself off, and continue.

I remember a sad day in December of 2003. December 22nd. That is when my oldest stepson's life journey ended at the young age of 20 as he was born February 27, 1983, and while his journey on Earth came to an end, his eternal journey just began.

There continues to be speculation about the cause of his death, but the one common thing is that his use of drugs played a role. He wasn't defined as a "druggie" which of course was one of his struggles, but as Derek, a son, stepson, brother, friend to many, and an uncle to a niece who was born four months before his passing. He called her "a gem."

Sadly, all, or at least most, of us have one thing in common and that is we all have lost someone close to us to death, and I have come to realize that we never really "get over" someone's passing, but we eventually "accept it." I am still not over my dad's passing who died over twenty years ago, or Derek's passing, going on 19 years ago, but have accepted both.

Even as I am writing this with tears streaming down my cheek on March 8, 2022, my stepdaughter, who I love very much, lost her husband, Steve Davis, early this morning. The day before she enters into another year of her own life journey. Brittany got me a mug that doesn't call me her stepdad, but bonus dad.

While I value that cup, I really appreciate her bringing Steve, or as he is affectionately known by loved ones as Ebie, into her family's life journey.

While Ebie's journey concluded on this earth, his eternal journey is just beginning. As I have done before, I now find myself tearfully reflecting on the many good memories and influences Ebie has left me with in my journey, and thank you very much!

As I age, I am beginning to see that old man, who often wants to have alone time even when family and others are around, and I find myself slipping outside during family get-togethers, which can understandably be frustrating to others. The very first person to join me outside has been my dear friend Ebie, and never once did he say those words, "you need to come in there with everyone else," but instead he and I talked about anything and everything. He simply understood and valued mine and his time together.

While technically Ebie is my stepson-in-law, I guess I think of him as more like a brother. He and Brittany met as adults and did marry, and you see, Ebie was a little farther along in his journey than Brittany, but both adults grabbed onto the happiness they deserved and walked side by side as they continued on in their journeys.

While I liken him to a brother, what is different about our brotherly relationship is that we never quarreled or argued, which brothers inevitably do sometimes. I remember Ebie as being understanding, very kindhearted, and extremely helpful.

What has helped me accept my dad's passing and my stepson's passing is continuing to have the memories and influences they left me with when our journeys in life merged or brought us together. Those never die off but continue to live with me, and I will find the strength to eventually accept the passing of my dear friend Ebie, and he has been a great part of my own journey. God bless you, Ebie, and love you, man.

Hearing my seven-year-old grandson cry when he learned of Ebie's passing breaks my heart. Ebie called him hot rod. His sadness and pain takes me back to my first encounter with death when I was only five ,and you will learn more about that encounter as you read on.

Well, Malek, or as we call him, Meeky, Pappy will be here for you to help you with this difficult moment in your young life. I love you very much!

I can look back at different times in my 56 year life journey and remember the great times, sad and tough times, and the different people I have met along the way, and the impact they had on me, and yes, the impact I had on them again; just like in travels, we often bring home souvenirs, and everyone I have had a friendship with in my life journey is a true souvenir for me.

If you happen to be one of those people, as you read this, you might get some insight into why I was the way I was, and why I am the way I am now. I am blessed to be able to say that I have had a lot of great relationships with people, but let's be real: while most of my relationships have been great and rewarding, all of us would have to admit that we all, me included, have had toxic or not so good relationships also.

Thanks to Google, I learned the exact day my life journey began and that was on a Sunday December 5, 1965 when that lady (TL) gave birth to me. This past Sunday, December 5, 2021, marks the 56th year in my journey.

You will learn why I refer to the lady who gave birth to me as that lady instead of Mom. That title Mom isn't to be taken lightly but is earned, and I do have a mother, who as you will see, did earn that title, Mother.

Well, that lady had my brother and sister two years before me, and my three other siblings after me. My older brother, sister, and I met up with that lady, and again, you will learn why I say met up with, later on in our journeys, and two of my brothers and I have had rare phone conversations later on in life, and at one point as she was nearing the end of her own journey, she said she won a settlement from a lawsuit where she slipped and fell on a wet floor and she said she was going to give each of us some money, and now that her journey has ended, not surprisingly, we haven't seen a penny, and quite frankly, I am glad. I have worked for and earned things in my life on my own and didn't rely on that lady.

Well, my brothers laugh and joke about us not getting money or wooden crosses, which she also promised, and even though she didn't give us these wooden crosses, she did give us figurative wooden crosses to carry during much of our life journeys.

While we don't have anything tangible from that lady, we do have a lot of memories or what I refer to as emotional scars, and I hope that by sharing these memories, others who have and are currently experiencing traumas can see they too can move forward in life, picking themselves up, brushing themselves off, and continuing on.

I have found that while life is a journey, it is unlike a journey in a vehicle as there is no reverse, but we move forward with turns along the way.

Before I share my life story full of emotional scars, I will talk about another reason I am ready to tell my story and that is due to two heartbreaking and shocking events that happened in this small Ohio County I reside and work in.

You will learn that I was in the custody of Columbiana County Ohio child protective services for close to two years. Think of that title, "child protective services," and you would think that such an agency would rescue and offer refuge to abused children. Well, over the past few years, there were two children that died while in services with child protective services.

One was a baby found dead at the bottom of a well and another a five-year-old. Both died as clients of CPS in this small Ohio County. One wasn't even allowed to start his journey and another's journey ended when she was five years old. I would like to think that they are both now in the hands of the one person who is truly a protector of children, and that is Jesus Christ.

CPS has changed or evolved from the days I was in their care in the early seventies, and now it seems their goal is to keep families together. They even have visits for children in their care with persons who continue to be in one way or another a part of the environment they were removed or rescued from.

When I was in the care of CPS, and granted, I was young, I don't recall having visits nor do I think there was ever the option of placing me back with biological relatives, but instead with persons who truly wanted to be parents and in an environment which afforded me opportunities to move forward in life.

It wasn't about that lady, but about me and my siblings or the children. I would pose the question, is today's CPS mission in Ohio about the child or about the adult they are charged with protecting the child from?

My wife told me 18 years ago that it isn't about me but about my granddaughter, and that remains true with my other grandchildren, great granddaughter, and stepchildren, no matter how far along they are in their own journeys.

Life journeys are like actual journeys, and I remember times when I have traveled before and was thankful for help from others who have traveled to that destination before for giving me tips on how to get there.

Life journeys are no different. As the seasoned travelers, so to speak, it is up to us adults to guide the younger travelers in their life journeys. What a wonderful responsibility.

Having said that, I especially want to tell this story of my own life journey to my three grandchildren, Jaden Malone, Malek Malone, and Prince Malone, as well as my great granddaughter, Skylar Linne. Bon voyage!

I would also like to say to my stepson, who is going through his own struggles, that you too can and will pick yourself up with help from those of us that love you and move forward in your long life journey ahead. You're going to be scarred, but the memories of those scars will affect how you make better decisions in the future.

I have heard the term "emotional scars" a lot throughout my life, and as you know, I am a 56 year old man with a wonderful wife, a stepdaughter who I am blessed to have, a stepson (love ya, man—that's our saying), a late stepson, may he Rest In Peace, a granddaughter who has given me a lot of happiness and great memories, a grandson who is doing the same, another grandson who I am bonding with and look forward to getting to know, my great granddaughter, and I am watching the family continue to grow. Oh, and I am a licensed social worker who has been at a mental health clinic for over 25 years. That's me, and yeah, I have a lot of physical scars from careless acts and from being a klutz.

I love doing as much as I can by myself, a DIYer, I guess, which means I have tried my hand at carpentry, mechanical work, electrical work, plumbing, and other jobs. I love being able to say I did it, but yeah, I have some visible scars from being a handyman. I have a scar on the base of my left thumb, and when I look at it, I think back to the day I was working on my riding lawn mower and put my hand over the carburetor; after all, I have seen mechanics choke a carburetor by putting their hand over it. Here's the thing though, the engine was running on the mower when I covered the carburetor, and there was what looked like a plastic fan blade spinning around, and ouch, a blade from it broke off in my thumb. It was a painful, bloody mess that led me to the ER and referred to a hand surgeon, who was able to remove the piece. Years later, when I think about it, the pain and blood are gone, and yeah, I can laugh, look at that scar, and say I will never do that again.

I remember working on my bathroom floor and using a skill saw to cut plywood. I have been using this type of saw for a while, and why take time to carry a piece of plywood to sawhorses, so I propped an end of plywood over my right thigh to get it up off the floor and cut it, and OUCH, the blade cut through my thigh. Thankfully, it didn't cut so deep that it did irreparable damage, but it was another trip to ER and more stitches. I look at that scar and say I will never do that again.

When it comes to ladders, it has taken me a long time to learn and play it safer. I have lost count of the number of falls, broken and fractured bones, and bruises. One scar on my left ankle has finally got me to play it safe. You see, I was screwed (in my left ankle that is) to repair it after falling with an extension ladder.

I had this habit of putting the extension ladder on a wet wooden deck and the laws of physics worked cause when I reached the top of the ladder the bottom fell out. I play it much safer now. I can see all the battle scars I have, laugh, and say I'll never do that again and while the pain, blood, and bruises are long gone I'd like to say I am a much safer do it yourselfer.

The way I see it physical scars are visible even as the body grows. I have a scar very near my left eyebrow from an injury sustained before the age of five. I have emotional scars too and the difference is they aren't physically visible, except maybe the physical scar near my eyebrow. Emotional scars like physical scars have lasting memories attached to them, and while I can laugh about the memories of my physical scars as humorous as I like to be, I find it difficult to laugh about my emotional scars and while it isn't pleasant reflecting on how I got them, the memories are there nonetheless.

Before I talk about my own emotional scars, I want to point out that many of us share similar emotional scars. You know the saying I remember where I was when… JFK was assassinated, Elvis died, the attempted assassination of Ronald Reagan, and the day the twin towers fell on 9/11. Someday we will all remember the era of the COVID pandemic as well.

To demonstrate my opinion of emotional scars which more than likely most of us have I am going to share my own emotional scars or those moments I wish I wouldn't have to remember.

I introduced myself at the beginning in as far as where I am at in life today, and now I want to share where I started out 56 years ago, and as you know I was born on Sunday, December 5, 1965 in Mansfield, Ohio as Ronnie, and I will not mention the last name I was born with, but as an aside, I am guessing it could've been an icy day. I am proud to say though that when I was seven years old, I officially became Jonathan Pariseau when I was thankfully adopted by my late mother and father, Dennis and Donna Pariseau, for reasons you will soon discover.

As I said earlier, I am going to refer to the lady that gave birth to me as that lady or TL. Yeah, she carried me for nine months and delivered me when she was 24 years into her own life journey.

At first glance, a person would think that lady really loved children and really wanted to be a mom, but that is far from the truth. You see, I was born the third child in December 1965, and TL's first child (my sister) was born in November 1963, her second child (my brother) was born December 9, 1964. Since I was born the following year on December fifth before his first birthday, he and I are the same age for three days, and then he reclaims the title of older brother. One of my other brothers was born in January of 1967, and my youngest brother was born again in December four years later (five years after me).

The first five years of my life are full of emotional scars or things I can remember even before the age of five. I would argue that I shouldn't have to remember these things. I have asked my seven-year-old grandson if he remembers when he and I went to the fair when he was four, and he says no. Sad, because we had a good time, but if something traumatic were to have happened, he probably would sadly remember.

I have a lot of memories before the age of five of being locked in rooms such as the basement and bedrooms with my three siblings by TL and who knows where she was at or what she was doing while she imprisoned four children she brought into this world. One can only imagine.

I remember one time being locked in the basement with my three siblings and me, being under five, I am guessing the oldest couldn't have been older than six, and therefore there are four very young and impulsive children locked in a basement for what seemed like an eternity, and we lacked decision-making skills.

I remember being bored and looking for ways to have fun, and while I compare that time in the basement to being imprisoned it was different in that there were no guards there to supervise. Wow, four young children left alone for hours on end what possibly could go wrong?

I was able to encourage my brother who is a year younger than me to do risky and rotten behaviors at times. After all, acting up isn't as fun alone as it is with your partner in crime or PIC. PIC is who I will refer to my younger brother from this point on. PIC and I had several adventures in the garden, and of course, our grandfather who planted and tended to the garden had one rule—no kids unattended allowed. Oops, PIC and I overlooked that rule and we picked tomatoes and threw them at who knows what or even who.

Back to the basement (words I heard a lot as a young boy). Like I said, I wanted to have fun, so PIC and I ran around playing chase when I came up with an idea of having PIC get on my shoulders and me running with him, but upped the ante. We found some good things that could be used as blindfolds (socks, shirts, etc.). Two children both, under five with one running with the other one on his shoulder and both blindfolded, what could possibly go wrong? You have seen those metal posts used as support braces in basements, and one of those posts put an end to my and PIC's fun. After all, we didn't see it.

When that lady finally opened the basement door, she discovered PIC and I crying in pain, with bloody foreheads. She took us on our first trip to the ER, which, as you know, would be one of many for me. The ER cleaned us up and stitched us up ironically above both of our eyebrows. Remember the scar near my left eyebrow? That's my memory attached to that scar. Will never do that again, and more importantly as a responsible and mature adult (at least in my opinion) would never let my grandchildren do that either.

There was another time when TL locked PIC and I in a bedroom. Were babysitters not invented in the sixties? What a stupid move to lock PIC and I up in a room again for what seemed like an eternity with no food, water, or bathroom. We did have a bed though, but napping was the farthest thing from our minds, or at least mine. We found creative ways to spend our time. Art and crafts with two toddlers.

TL would never have expected to see the mess when she opened the door. Remember there wasn't a bathroom, and let's just say Mother Nature took her course. You can put Mother Nature on hold, but you can't hang up. PIC may have been in a diaper, even. I'll let your imagination go crazy on what TL was welcomed home with.

Looking back, I guess I was a bit of a handful for TL. There was a time when she and I were in the kitchen alone and she was cooking. I know that but not what she was cooking. Aww, I guess any child would have fond memories of being with their mother in the kitchen; after all, I remember seeing my wife in the kitchen with her children, and now with our grandchildren. I have learned you have to be patient with them and show them the proper way to do things, but that's not the memory I have of being in the kitchen with that lady.

Here is the thing I must have done something to upset her (not me). I can't remember what I did, but I do remember her response. She grabbed my head, and with a hand on each side proceeded, to bang my head against the wall for what seemed like forever, and finally stopped after one of my teeth fell out.

I want to talk about that three-letter word that starts with s and ends with x, and try to answer the question of who that man is; after all, that lady needed that man (TM) to bring me into this world, and here's the thing, I honestly don't know who that man is, but then again I really don't care, because I do know who THE MAN is. Remember, Dennis Pariseau, my father, who adopted me when I was seven?

I remember a man in the home who went to work at a pottery factory in East Liverpool, Ohio where we lived for the first five years of my life, and I remember the police coming to the house more than once and taking him to jail, and then him coming home from jail. I hear this man may be responsible for one or two of my siblings, but not necessarily my two younger siblings and me. There is even some talk that some of his brothers may have contributed. I guess everyone knew but that man.

I do know that TM's dad lived in the home with us, and I affectionately referred to him as Paps. Nowadays, I am known as Pappy. The majority of my fond moments of my first five years are with Paps up to August 9, 1971, when he passed away, shortly before I turned six years old. Paps took me under his wings. Every little boy needs a man to teach them simple things, like how to go pee pee, even and he was that man for me. He even taught me how to dry my back with a towel after bathing. I followed him with my plastic lawnmower. Paps worked at a convenient store within walking distance from the house, and he would always come home with my favorite life savers. He knew my and PIC's connection and brought some for him too. I remember him coming home, and PIC and I running up to him and checking his pockets, and we always found two packages of Life Savers, and believe it or not, we split them. One pack each.

Those days ended in August 1971 when he passed on. I learned about it in the middle of the night when that lady woke me up and told me Paps died, and that being my first experience with death, I learned it meant he was no longer on this earth. I remember her saying to me when I was crying that he wanted me to have his watch. I guess he was teaching me to tell time, but guess what, TL never gave me his watch. To this day, I have no idea what happened to it.

Yeah, I have a lot of good memories of Paps, but he also left me with an emotional scar. Remember when I asked my grandson if he remembers our trip to the fair when he was four and he doesn't? Well, I remember mine and Pap's trip to the fair when I was four. He took PIC and me to the fair, and while I don't remember all the rides we rode or the games we played, I do remember one ride we rode after Paps beat the you-know-what out of the ride operator to get us on that ride.

The operator wasn't going to let us on the ride. I guess we were too short. Paps really wanted us to be able to ride it, so he beat him into submission. The young man operated the ride while PIC and I rode it, but I couldn't really enjoy the ride because of what I had just seen, and looking at the operator bleeding made me sick to my stomach.

Looking back, I guess Paps played a bigger role in that house with TL and four young children. I guess TL never did learn a lesson, so to speak, because after Pap's death in August, she gave birth to my youngest brother that December. Now that I have learned some things about pregnancy, I now know she was pregnant with him when Paps died.

Four kids are a lot, but I guess five was a bit much, because not too long after my little brother was born, that lady literally left and yes. without the five children she brought into this world. My older brother, sister, PIC, and I all have our own memories of that day when TL flew the coop so to speak, but here's my memory.

I remember it being a decent day with no rain, and I am guessing it was a spring day. All five of us children were outside, and I don't remember what or if anything TL said to us before she drove off, but I remember her giving all of us a balloon and then driving off. She certainly was symbolic, because remember her saying to my brothers that she wanted to give us wooden crosses, and while we didn't literally get those, we already figuratively carried our own crosses through life?

Well, I am sure I let go of my balloon, and it soared high and moved freely, and that is what I was able to do in my own life journey after finally being able to lay down the weight of that cross.

I thought that lady drove off alone, but my older brother has said he recalls seeing a man lying in the back seat. I guess he checked out the car, but anyway, that was the last time I saw that lady until 16 years later after I graduated from college and decided to meet up with her once again, only that time I wasn't a vulnerable, needy, young boy, but a grownup.

Back to that day when TL drove off leaving five children she brought into this world outside like unwanted belongings left at the curbside for disposal. I guess she locked up the house, so I remember my older sister and brother getting mad at me because I was laughing. Better laugh than cry I guess, but my brother and sister didn't find anything funny about all of us being locked out of the house and left outside. Here is the thing though, I have reflected on that day a lot, and now that I think about it, after locking us up in different rooms in the house TL locked us out of the house or out in the world to fend for ourselves, and I found that to be a reason to laugh or be happy.

We didn't have to fend long though, because by nightfall we were with relatives. I guess word got out that there were five abandoned children. Before being rescued, my older brother's memory of that day is we ended up in the house, which may be true. I guess breaking into a house may have become a useful skill for at least one of us children.

He also remembers my sister using trash bags as diapers for the baby among us. I can't blame her, and how ingenious. No matter how much my sister may have tried her hand at mothering for one day, and she probably did much better than TL, we needed adult supervision, and that is what we had at the end of the day.

I often wonder where that man in the house was, because the man that my brother saw lying in the back of the car wasn't that man, and from what I hear, he wasn't even of the same race. I am guessing that man in that house in East Liverpool was doing some more time in jail when TL left, and I remember us children staying with at least three different relatives for awhile, and being left with a couple more emotional scars.

One night I remember being in bed at my aunt's house and there being a commotion outside, and even seeing the lights from sirens. It was hard to sleep, but I did my best, and when I finally awoke, and went downstairs to my aunt pouring me a bowl of cereal, I learned what happened. She was still in pain and suffering from having all her teeth punched out by that lady, and I am assuming TL may have joined that man in jail. What was her thing with teeth? Remember, she knocked one of my teeth out one time, and if she didn't want us, why assault a lady for stepping in and helping out?

Well, I guess an uncle stepped up to help as well, because I remember being at his place, and that man must have gotten his get out of jail free card, because he showed up at the door, and my uncle met him and they exchanged words. Little ole me decided to go to the door where they were and my uncle grabbed ahold of my black curly hair, picked me up off the floor, and threw me across the room where I landed on a couch. I now think that my uncle may have been that man's brother, and since there is the question of who contributed to bringing us children into the world, he could possibly have been a contributor for one at least, and wasn't wanting to let lose, but thankfully he did.

I remember Grandmother even trying to fill the void, but eventually Columbiana County Ohio child protective services stepped in and placed all five of us children in foster care. At that time, it seemed like forever that we were in foster homes, because I was in at least three different homes and a children's home as well, but I guess it may have been close to two years, and now at this point in life, two years seems like two days, but not back then.

Not all five of us were placed in homes together. Remember PIC? That was the last time I saw him for close to two years, because they placed him and my older brother in homes together, and me and my sister in homes together. I couldn't imagine any foster parent being able to handle PIC and me anyway.

I remember my sister and me being in a children's home with what seemed like thousands of other children and two house parents, and one afternoon the house dad I guess came to me and told me to go with him, and I ran and yelled and cried, saying I didn't want to go. I even laid on the ground and grabbed ahold of a flagpole and he tried pulling me off, and when my sister heard me carrying on, she intervened but to no avail. I ended up going with the man, and I guess that incident caused my sister and me to be separated, because she and I were placed together in two different foster homes before they separated us and placed me in what was to be my last foster home.

Being all alone, I remember crying myself to sleep at times, but I survived. I had a foster brother and while no one could replace PIC, I sure have a few memories of me and my foster brother. He and I were on a same baseball team for kids our age. I loved it, uniforms and all. One day, he and I were at a game and my foster parents weren't there to watch. Good thing, because neither he nor I got in the game. He was a bit more disappointed than me because my foster parents were literally his parents.

While our uniforms were sparkling clean, I noticed that the star players' uniforms were not. I guess they got dirty from things like sliding. I came up with this idea of foster brother and me rolling around in a dirt patch to make it look like we played, and while everyone around looked at us with bewilderment, I guess it worked because my foster brother's parents thought we played, and his mother had to wash our uniforms not knowing we could've returned with pristine clean ones. Oops.

I remember a time when my foster parents took us to a drive-in theater. Those were the days. Cars lined up watching a movie on a big screen. I guess people got in for free just by being smuggled in the trunk until they parked to watch the movie. Well, my foster father was no different. He and his wife had a son, daughter, foster son, and foster daughter. While I can't remember the movie we watched, I do remember my foster sister and me being the two locked in the trunk in order to spare a buck or two. I'd like to think that if he had known all the times I had been locked up, he wouldn't have done that.

Remember the pastor's words, "we all have a story to tell," and me believing I have a responsibility to share my journey? Now I guess will be the most difficult part of fulfilling that responsibility and I think I am now ready to do so.

As a social worker, I see and talk to people who have suffered physical and emotional abuse as well as neglect, and from everything I've shared, I don't think anyone would disagree when I say I as a very young child suffered neglect, physical, and emotional abuse, but you see, I have also talked to people who have been the victim of sexual abuse, and have even listened to adult women and men recount their own experiences as being a victim of sexual abuse, and then say with a sense of relief, "You are the first person I have told that to." Admiring their strength and willingness to do so, I reminded them that they aren't defined as being a victim, but as being a survivor. You see, who in their right mind would volunteer to go through almost seven years of what I endured. I didn't ask for it either, but I went through it. Victims don't ask for it, perpetrators do it, and survivors move on and live their lives free of the perpetrators.

Now that I have said this in honor of everyone who found the strength and courage to talk to me about their own experiences of having been sexually abused, I too did fall victim to sexual abuse when I was living in that last foster home. No, it wasn't by my foster parents unless you want to factor in their negligence. Remember my foster brother and me being at a baseball game by ourselves? Well, we were also at a basketball game by ourselves without my foster parents being there to supervise or look out for us, and an older boy took advantage of both me and my foster brother.

You would think that having been exposed to all the sports I was exposed to, I would be a great athlete, but I make a better carpenter than I do an athlete.

Now that I think about it, I really needed parents, not just foster or temporary parents, but real parents and guess what, in 1972 that's what I got, a mother and father and family.

I remember a day in 1972 when Dennis and Donna Pariseau picked up not only me but PIC, my older brother, and sister, and along with the three children they had already adopted, drove us to the big house on the top of a hill in Glen Roy, Ohio or Jackson County where I called home for eleven years up to the age of 18. Yeah, that large Pariseau family in Jackson County Ohio. You see, not only did they adopt three children, three of my siblings, and me,but also, four more siblings as well as other children. At last count, I think I am one of eighteen children when you count my two younger brothers who Donna gave birth to after she and Dad adopted several needy children. I have brothers and sisters of different races and we are family—a diverse family at that.

Now, back to the day that we were driving in that light blue van to a place I now call home. When we were going home, I was so excited I totally forgot that my baby brother wasn't in the van with us, so I asked Mom where he was, and she explained that she and Dad wanted to adopt him with us, but another couple adopted him because he was a baby. I am guessing he was united with his parents who I have since met and God bless them, even before Dennis and Donna adopted my other siblings and me.

I remember that first day in what seemed like a huge house at the time and being reunited with PIC, and right away he and I picked up where we left off and began exploring every inch of that house. We stumbled along a bunch of photos, and well, there were also scissors around, so we proceeded to cut up a lot of pictures. Well, after a while, Mom met up with us and amazingly seemed to understand that young, impulsive children will sometimes get into mischief, but she also let PIC and I know that our behaviors weren't acceptable, and while my older brother and sister enjoyed being at home that night, PIC and I were put to bed early in our bunk beds. You see, Dad built two triple bunk beds in one room. That was the first time I remember feeling bad for leading PIC astray.

Fast forward to 1984 when I graduated from Wellston High School among the top ten, listed in who's who among American high school students, giving a speech to the Rotary club one winter month when I was named senior of the month, and a member of the National Honor Society, and being accepted into Berea

College in Kentucky where I graduated with a BA degree.

I don't say all this to boast or brag on myself, but to point out that when I was adopted, Mom and Dad were told I was "retarded." I am guessing a social worker may have told them that, and here's the thing: as a social worker myself, I have learned not to jump to conclusions but to look at the whole picture, and while I will admit that having been to too many schools to count in close to a two-year period, that it was difficult to learn because every time I went to a different home, I also went to a different school. I can say I am not retarded.

I think that if I were to accept that label, that would be an insult and even an injustice to those that are legitimately retarded, and God bless them. Mom knew too that, even though I struggled as a young seven year old child, and was behind at least one, if not more than one, grade level, that I wasn't retarded and she got to work trying to get me caught up.

I remember evenings when she was cooking dinner, she would have me read from the *McGuffey's Eclectic Reading Series*, and by the time I finished reading the final book in the eight-book series, I think I had earned most improved student in elementary school and had even won a spelling bee or two. To be eclectic means to be diverse, and that I will accept.

While my mom was rightfully proud of the work she put in with me to get me to a point where I could use education as a tool to achieving goals, I don't know that anyone could be as proud as me. I remember Mom introducing me as a teenager to others as her "retarded son," and then pointing out that I am fluent in Spanish and a straight A student. Kinda embarrassing, but she wanted to be recognized I guess for her hard work.

Journeys can be exciting because of the unknowns or surprises along the way, and I learned that life journeys are no different.

I received a surprise this past November in my journey when one of the newest members of the SFHC Family, Kaitlin Colley, arrived. Kaitlin, who now works alongside me, recognized the name Pariseau, and asked me if I remember a Scott Dunn. Wow, my childhood friend, of course I remember him.

I remember one constant principal during my years at Coalton Elementary and then again at Wellston High School, and that is Mr. Dunn, as I referred to him, but his name is William or "Bill" Dunn. He was there when I was a struggling elementary student and was able to be there as I became what I would describe as an excellent academic high school student.

You see, Mr. Dunn wasn't just the one constant in my academic life as a child, but he and his wife, the late Monna Dunn, and son Scott Dunn were also very good friends of that large, diverse Pariseau family.

I remember Scott being an only child spending nights with my large family and me nights with him and his parents. We would go across the street and play in a creek until we heard his mom hollering for us to come eat. I think Scott may have said a couple times act like we didn't hear her.

Bill Dunn and my father Dennis had a great friendship, and now at my age, I better understand the value of adult friendships. Monna Dunn often cut my hair in her kitchen, and Dad and Bill Dunn shared scouting adventures with me, my brothers, and Scott.

Wow. the seventies at Coalton Elementary. and the early eighties at Wellston High School. and now it is 2022. Time really does fly by.

Well, Kaitlin went on to say that Scott is her dad, and her grandparents are Bill and Monna Dunn. Well, since then, I have had a chance to talk over the phone with Scott, and thanks to the technology we now have, have been able to exchange emails with my childhood principal Mr. Dunn or Bill, and Bill shared his memories of my parents, and here they are....

"I know the struggles they experienced raising so many children, I witnessed them doing without so you children could have. Their commitment was not to be taken lightly, they poured their heart and soul into it.

Remember the old school bus Denney put together to take the scout troop to Pennsylvania, the fun we had!

The station wagon your mother drove, not in the best shape but necessary for hauling all of you. She never missed a parent/teacher meeting for all of you and attended all PTO meetings along with Denney.

Wonderful times, wonderful memories". and added thanks "for the privilege of having known Denney and Donna Pariseau".

I did mention being fluent in Spanish, right, and I will spare sharing with you my wonderful experience of spending time in Madrid, Spain while in college, but wow, that was great, and I even got to visit a ER in Madrid (no surprise)!

You know that saying all good things too must come to an end? Well, my college years as good as they were, came to an end when I graduated, and after graduating, I worked a few jobs waiting tables and decided it was now time to meet up with that lady, and so I got ahold of my older brother, and got her contact information since he had already met her. I called her in Hermitage, Pennsylvania where she was living, and we talked on the phone. Eventually, I flew from Northern Kentucky where I was staying at the time to meet her and my teenaged half-sister. Wow, she had one last child before dying on June 2, 2015.

Well, I stayed a few days with TL, and the person I have come to know as Sis for a few days, and landed a job at a residential juvenile treatment center for boys, where I worked for several years before returning home to Jackson County, Ohio after Mom and Dad divorced.

I stayed with my mom and two younger brothers for a couple months before moving to Scioto County, Ohio where I have been working now for close to 30 years at Shawnee Family Health Center. A lot of changes can happen in 30 years. Shawnee Family Health Center was Shawnee Mental Health Center until we started with holistic healthcare, treating both physical and mental health, which makes sense because we all have both and both are closely connected.

A couple other changes since coming to Scioto County almost 30 years ago: I have since gotten my license as a Social Worker in the state of Ohio, and while I came here single, I have since met and married my wonderful wife, Kimberly Pariseau. She is awesome and I ask myself, how does she tolerate me?

I want to conclude this by saying why I decided to share my life events at this point in my life. I am approximately six years from retiring, and I have had years of opportunities to hear others talk about their own emotional scars and the effect those scars have had, and I want to share mine and how I have chosen to deal with them.

I remember several years ago talking to a gentleman who was my age at the time, and he lived alone, didn't work, but did volunteer. He told me that he had "abandonment issues" because when he was a child, his parents left him. I was thinking back and figured he and I would have been around the same age back then, and while I don't know the events that led up to his parents leaving, I could see a grown man who was still hurting from the event.

I pointed out to this gentleman that life is truly a journey, and unlike a trip in a vehicle, there is no reverse in life's journey, only forward with turns along the way, but I did learn that day when talking to this gentleman that there is a neutral in life's journey, because this person decided from that point in his young life that he was going to live in neutral. However, life continued to move on around him, and he, of course, like me aged because his adult body I am sure looks different than that of that young child.

Remember when I talked about meeting TL when I was in my early twenties? Well, she did offer an apology for the day she walked away, and I told her that she doesn't need to apologize to me. The person she needed to apologize to was that five year old boy, and that boy is no more.

I walked away from that meeting thanking God for being adopted and blessed to know that I have a younger sister who I have since reconnected with, and she too has a daughter, who is my niece.

My sis has shared with me her own I would say emotional scars from that lady she called Mom, and my niece knew her as Grandmother, and she was a devoted granddaughter. She has a lot of fond memories of her grandmother, and for that I am happy. I harbor no hatred for TL or my niece's grandmother, because to be frank, I don't know her life journey that at one point led to that day in December of 1965 when I was born, but I am guessing that she too had her own emotional scars.

While TL never would have been considered a candidate for mother of the year, it turns out that she was a good grandmother, and I am happy to hear that. After all, being a grandfather myself, I know all too well about the bond between a grandchild and grandparent, and I am glad my niece has those memories, and not the memories I have. Luv ya, niece.

Going back to the beginning when I talked about my collection of physical scars, well you see, I continue to enjoy taking on projects and doing as much as I can on my own. I still get on a ladder, pick up a hammer, and use a saw. But I would like to think I have learned a thing or two about safety.

I haven't let the emotional scars keep me from living either, but I have continued to live and enjoy the joys and challenges of being a parent, grandparent, and husband, and I am grateful to have worked in the career that I have worked in for close to thirty years now.

Finally, you know how I say my physical scars have taught me a bit about safety? Well, I have learned a thing or two from my emotional scars too, and that is actions do indeed speak much louder than words. You see, I don't remember much if anything that was said during my early years, but I certainly remember what was done.

I do believe there is good in all of us, and while we can say we love others, I have learned it is just as important, if not more important, to show love in our actions with others, especially the children who look to us adults for guidance as they begin their own life journeys.

To those of you who have intentionally brought a child into this world, please take his/her hand and walk with them in their journey, and if you "unintentionally" brought a child into this world and for whatever reason don't feel ready to or prepared for guiding that baby through life's journey, please consider letting someone else guide that child through his or her journey. It is not about you, but that precious child.

EXIT
SUPER BOWL
LVI
BENGALS